BUGS & INSECTS

ACTIVITY BOOK
FOR KIDS

This Book
Belongs To:

_____

_____

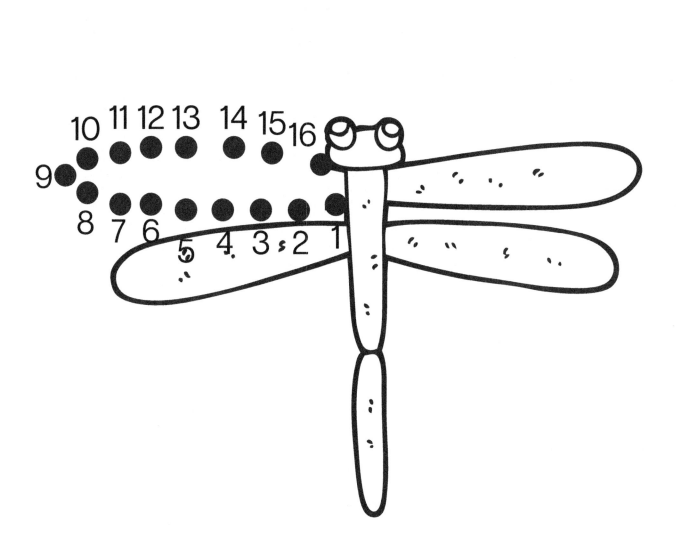

Help the bug
through the maze.

Word Search

Circle The Words Below

```
L U H N Y F U R T
N A E O P K G S D
A R D U W N L E F
D D A Y V I S L P
T R M I L T R D U
R D G A O S U D K
A C E H K U S A C
I U T U L E P S I
N H D C O R A T P
```

lady   made

stink   make

Count And Trace

1

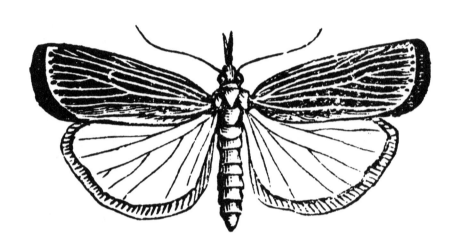

2

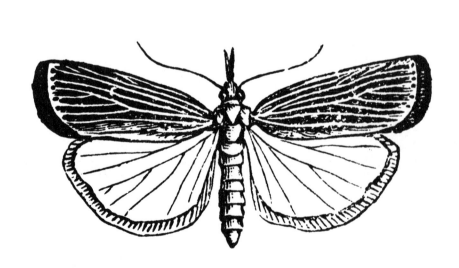

Spot The Difference

Count And Trace

1

2

3

4

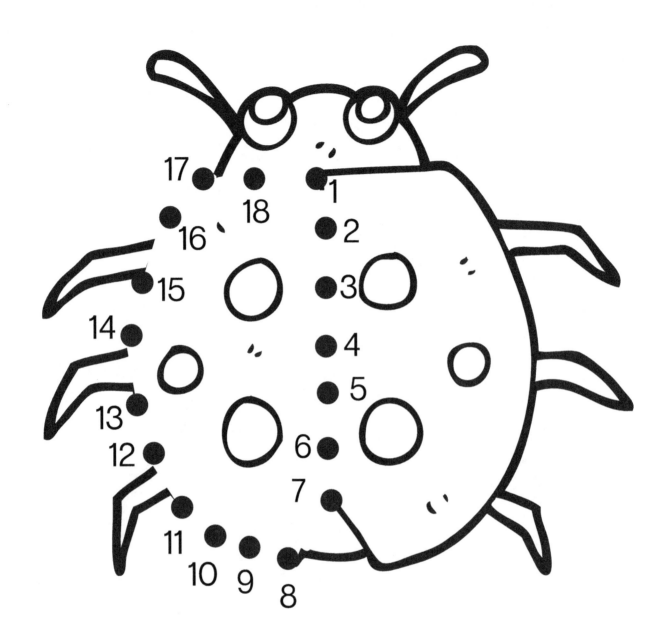

Help the bug
through the maze.

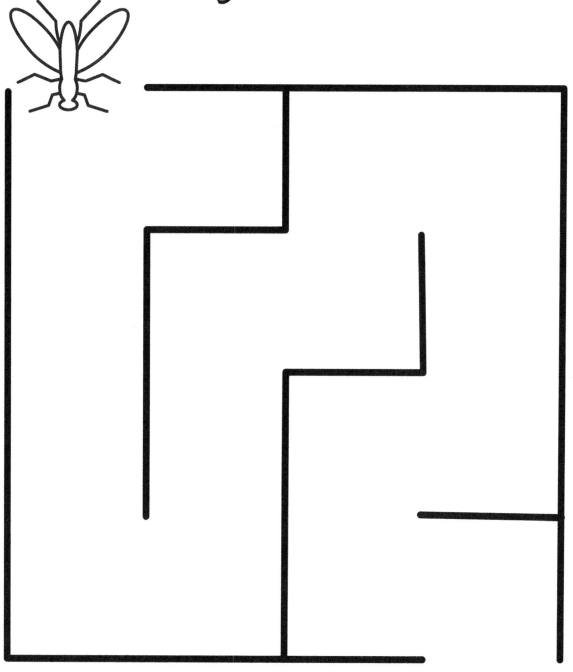

Word Search
Circle The Words Below

```
B U D N C L U R T
A S Q O S D P C B
S P H W E R E R A
N I A H O U T A R
D D F E E E E N N
O E T N E A U E A
C R E B F N N W L
K R R V L E T G O
C R I C K E T T E
```

spider   were

cricket   when

Count And Trace

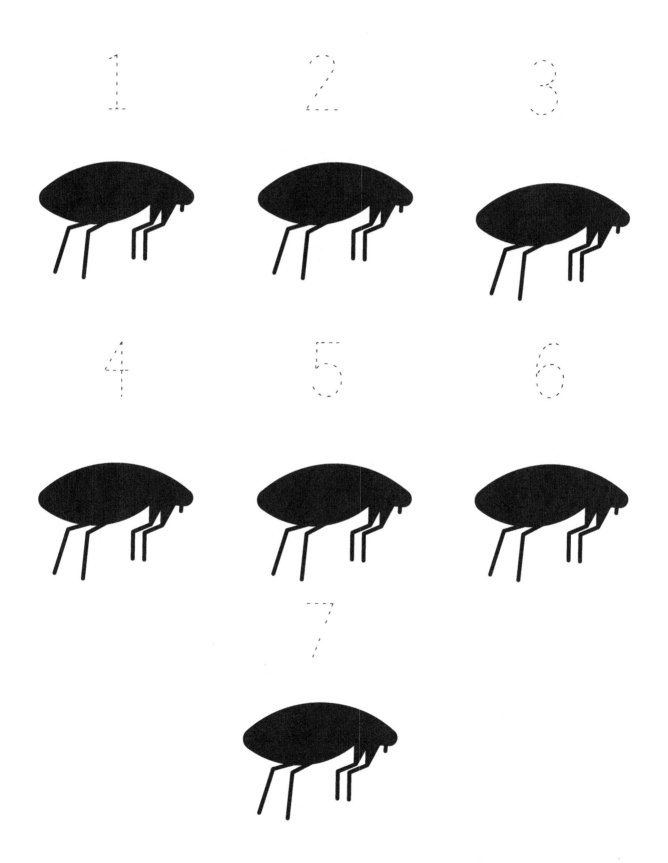

Spot The Difference

Count And Trace

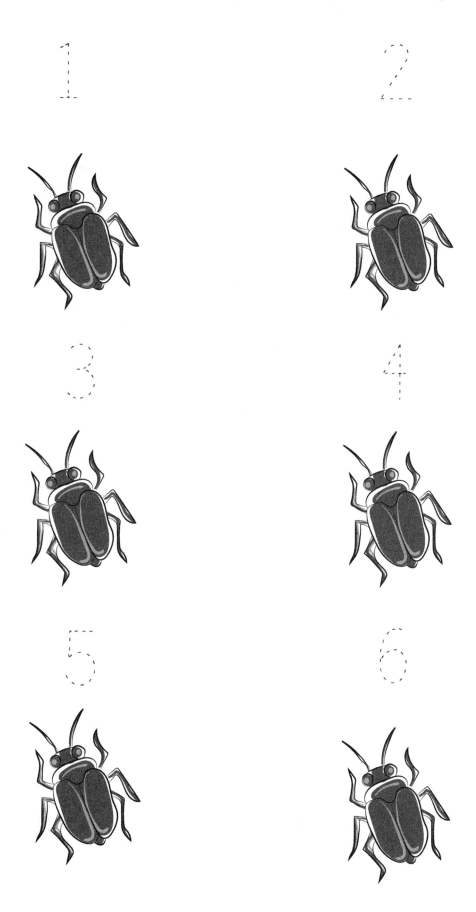

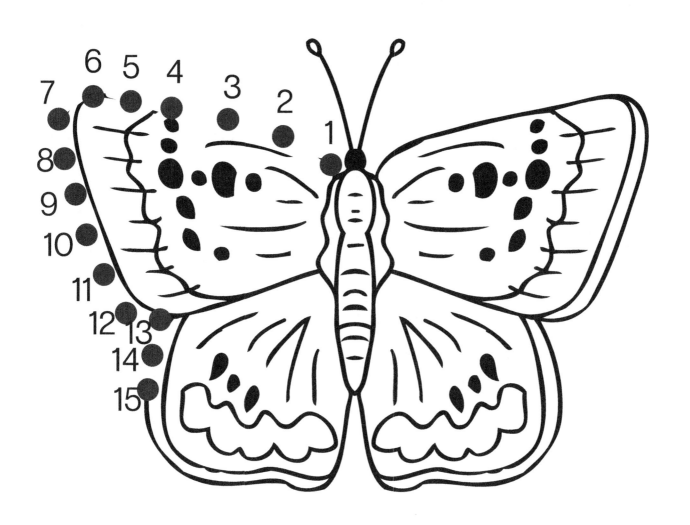

Help the bug through the maze.

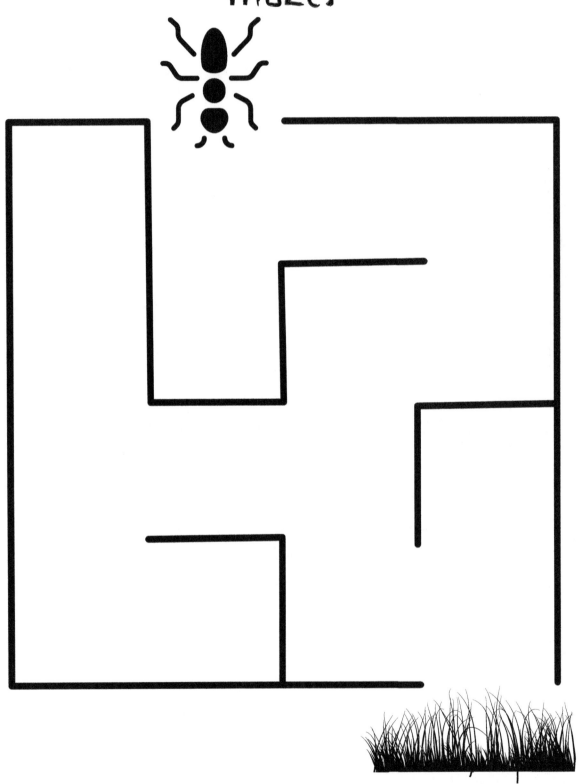

Word Search

Circle The Words Below

```
T U G N D F U R K
J O L E Y F I S C
S C E L L D L E O
G S N L F E H A T
R T E C N E D L S
A N E N I T L R E
S A B A R A U W V
S E A H O L O E I
C O H C I H W T L
```

ants   which

seed   would

Count And Trace

1

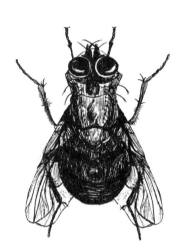

2

3

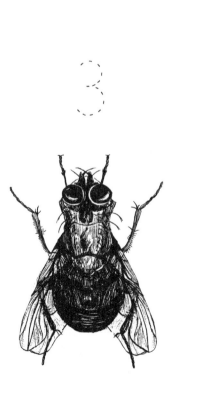

Spot The Differences

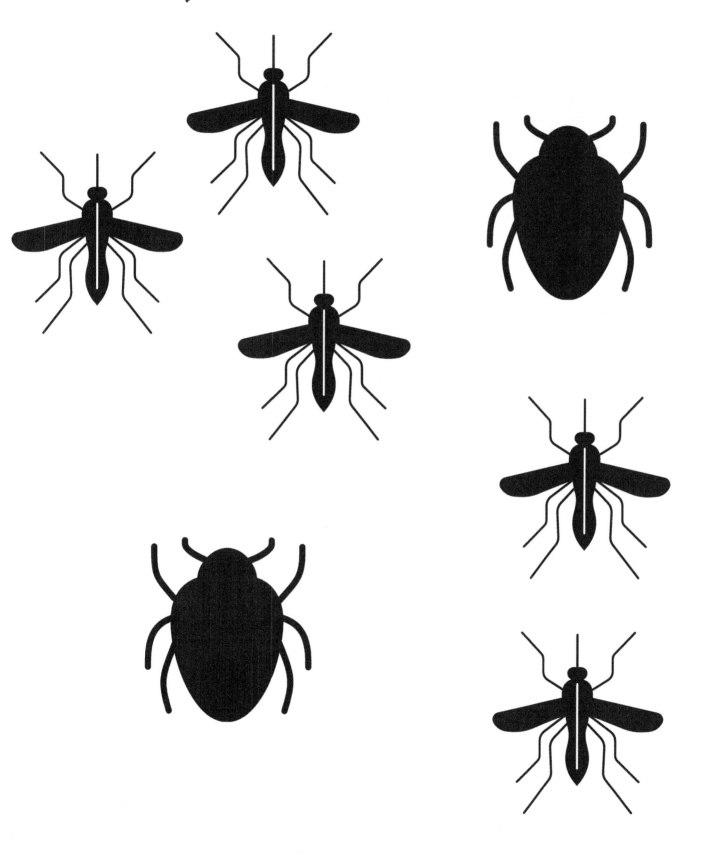

Count And Trace

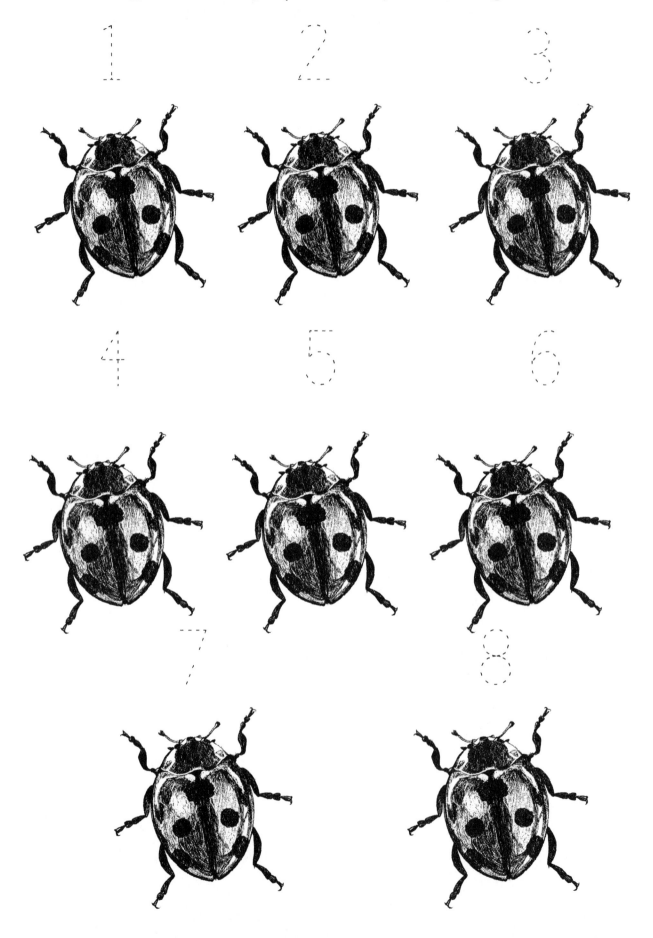

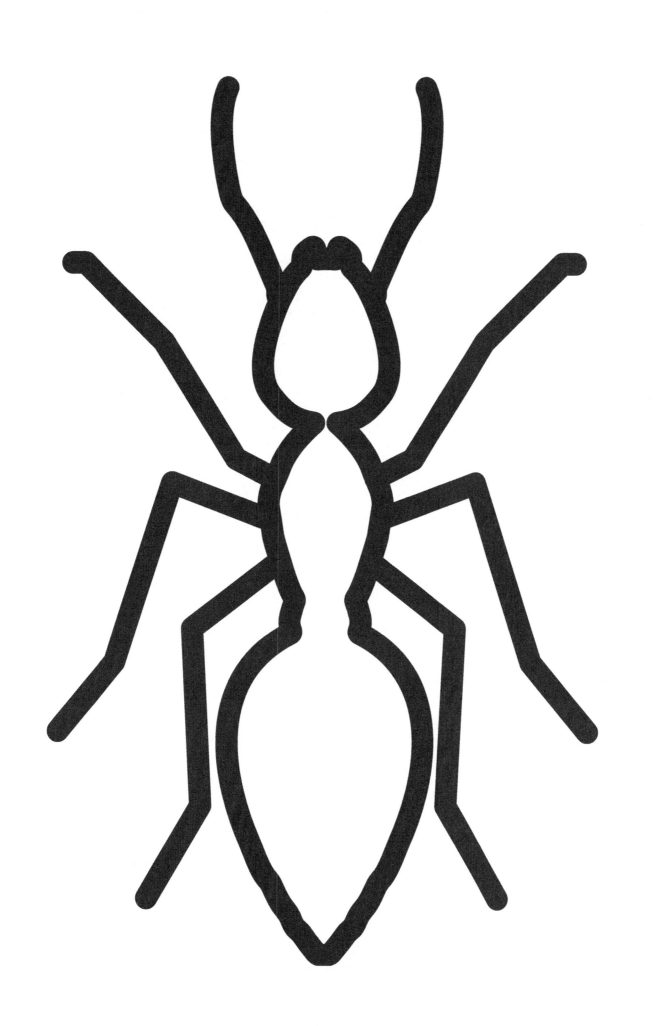

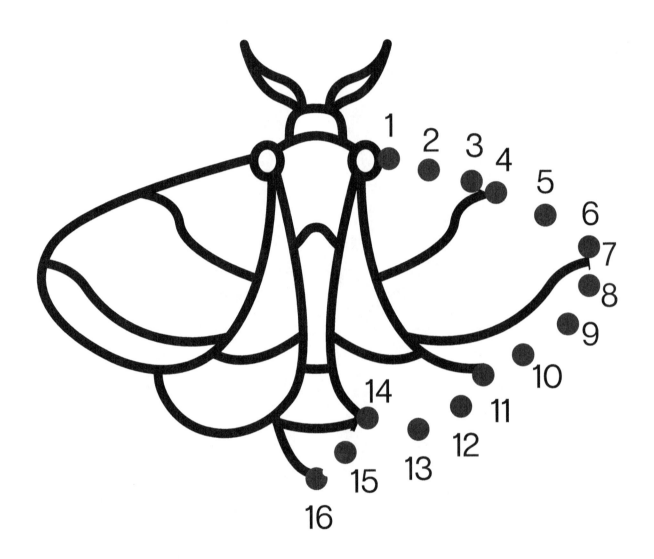

Help the bug
through the maze.

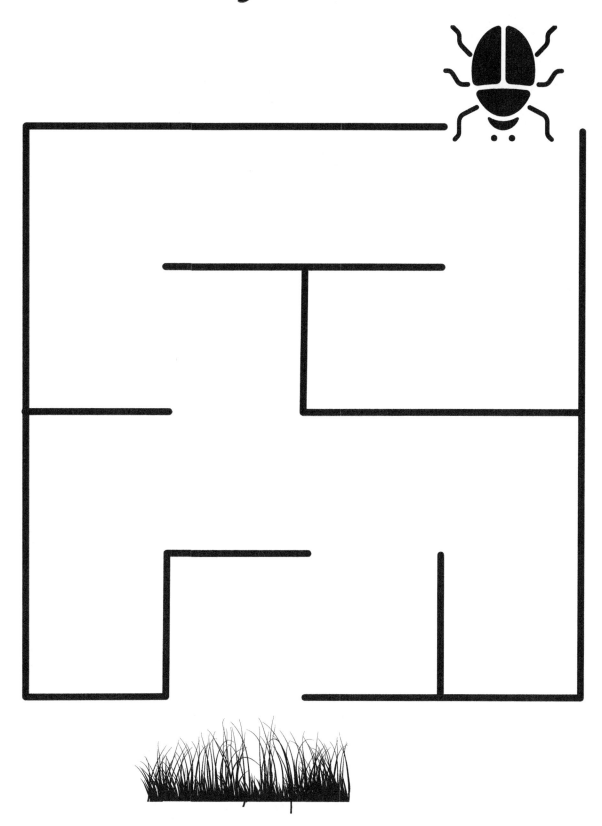

Word Search

Circle The Words Below

S W G N Y F U R B
B I X O R L E R I
F L L U U E L I S
L P N V E O E N O
Y D O E E P I N N
A D E R L R C D W
R F N Y R O P W E
K U L O R W T T R
C H D C F N A T E

fly   very

silver   use

Count And Trace

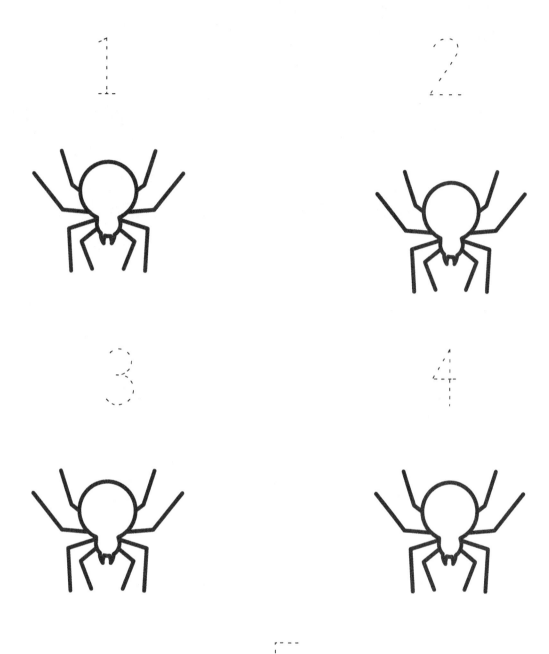

Spot The Difference

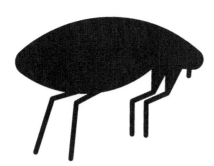 

 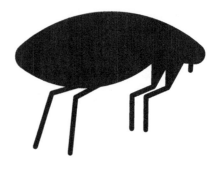

Count And Trace

1

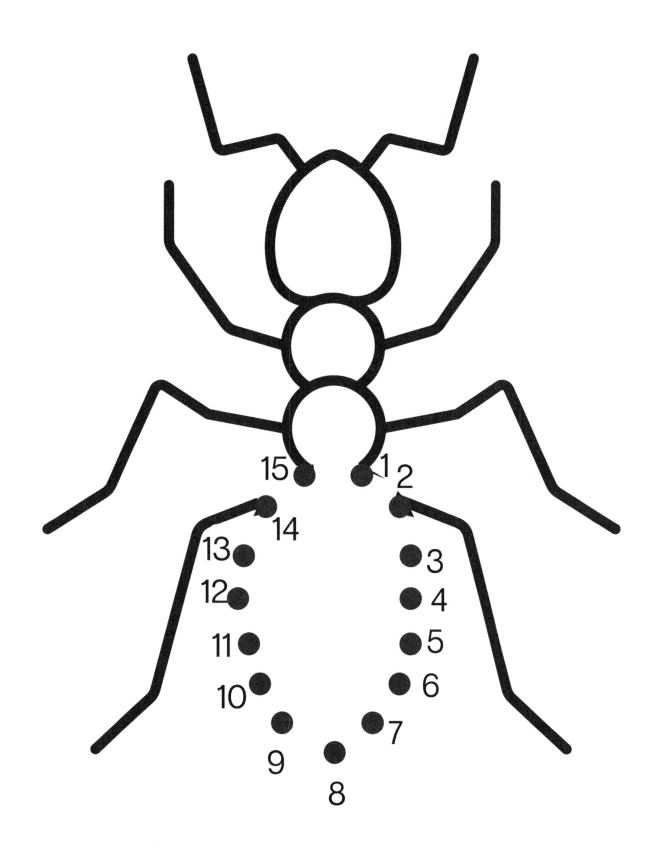

Help the bug through the maze.

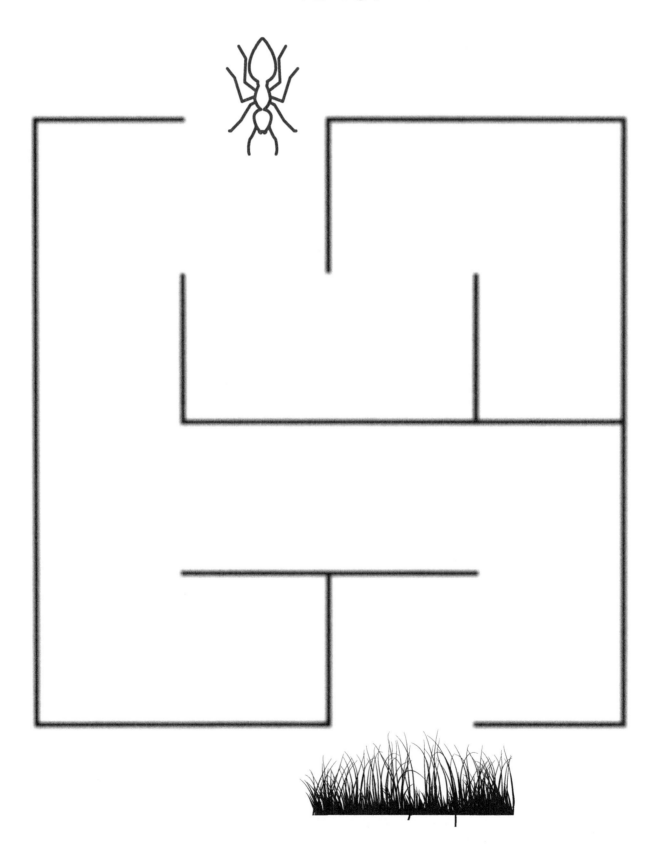

Word Search
Circle The Words Below

```
P S W H H I N O C
A A F C P N E E O
G G N A E T M A C
N A A B I T E R H
O F E E L U R L R
L O P D B B F O O
C X Y I I E N W A
K U T R N A P G C
G A R B A A G E H
```

bed   bite

cockroach   long

Count And Trace

Spot The Difference

Count And Trace

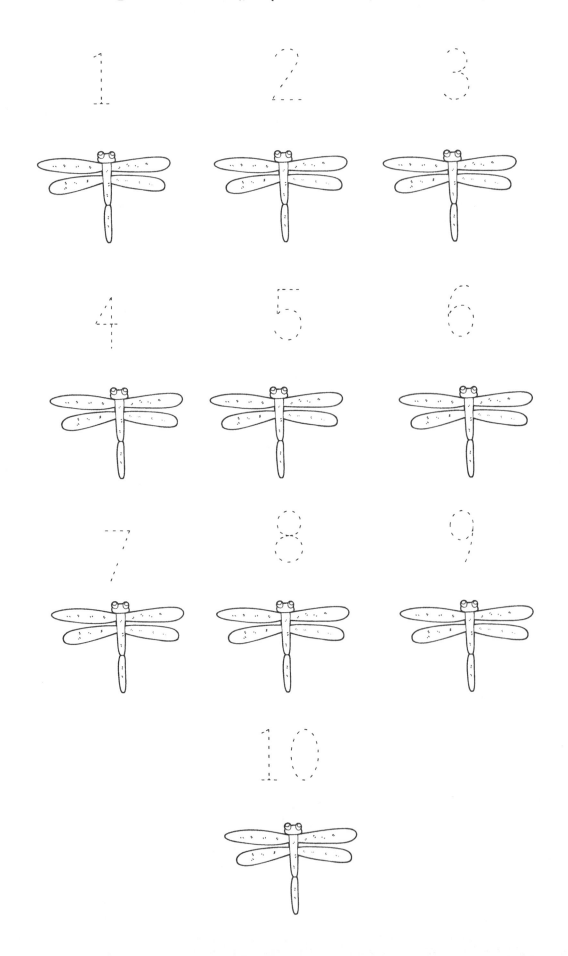

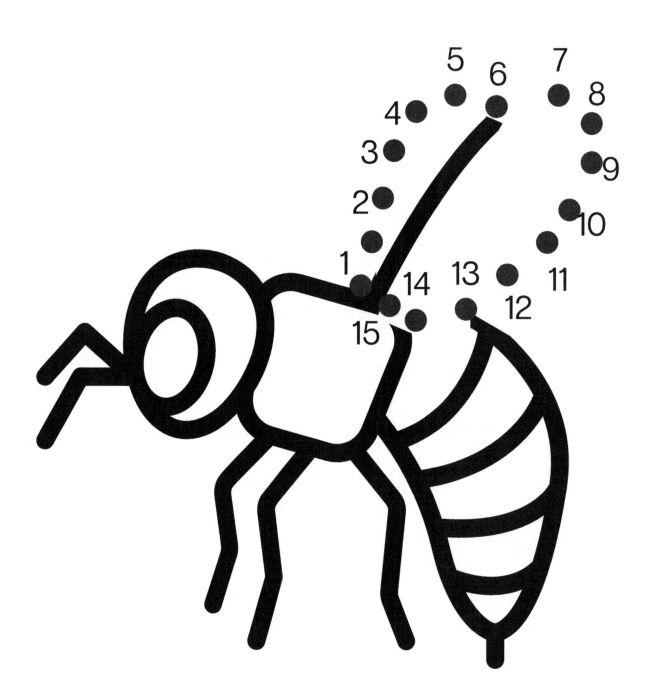

Help the bug
through the maze.

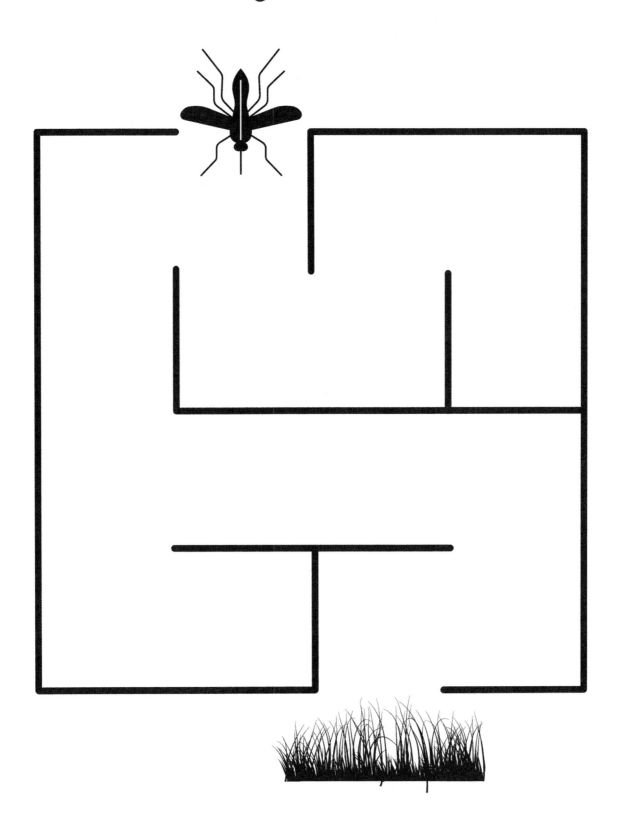

Word Search

Circle The Words Below

```
C E N T I P E D E R
R C A H F I N D H
E M A E I A Y I E
S A A B R L R Y E
S N R E S R E B T
A C A E T H R O A
G L C A T S T L H
E U N A D E S A R
C P F R T Y U T H
```

centipede   the

bee   they

COUNT AND TRACE

11

Spot The Difference

COUNT AND TRACE

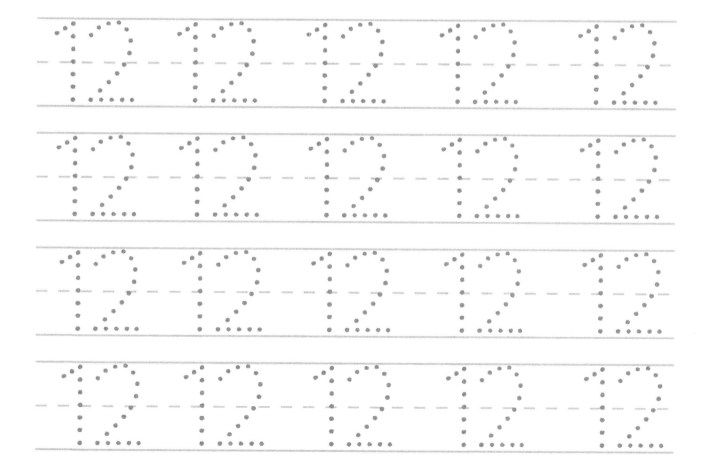

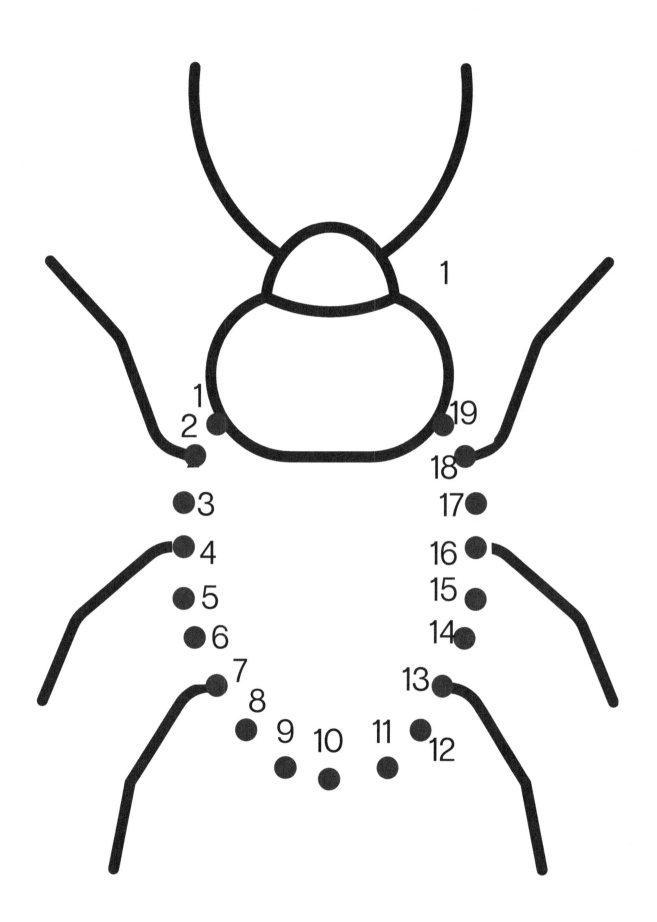

Word Search

Circle The Words Below

```
M I S E L T E E B
O S F R P W E F U
G A I T B E E T T
I W N R F E T N T
R N A R A V I B E
T O O S L I L O R
H I N F P L I W F
G F A I D S T G L
C H D T O R Y L Y
```

wasps   beetles

weevils   butterfly

Help the bug through the maze.

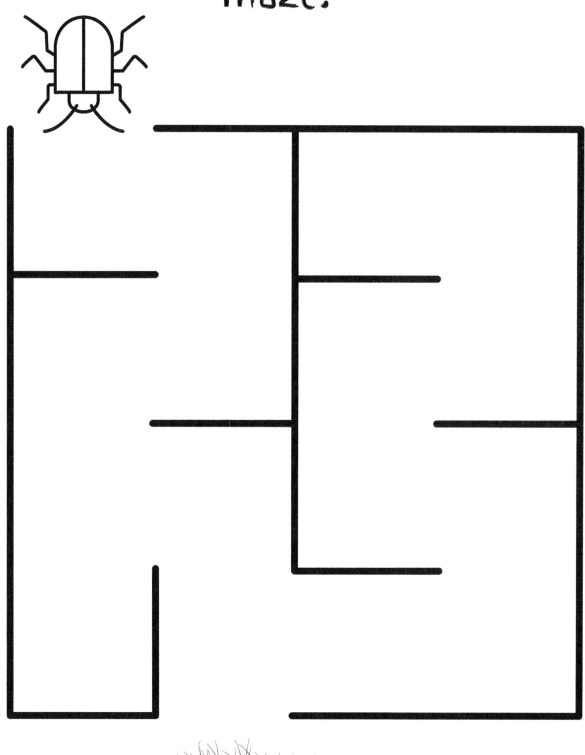

COUNT AND TRACE

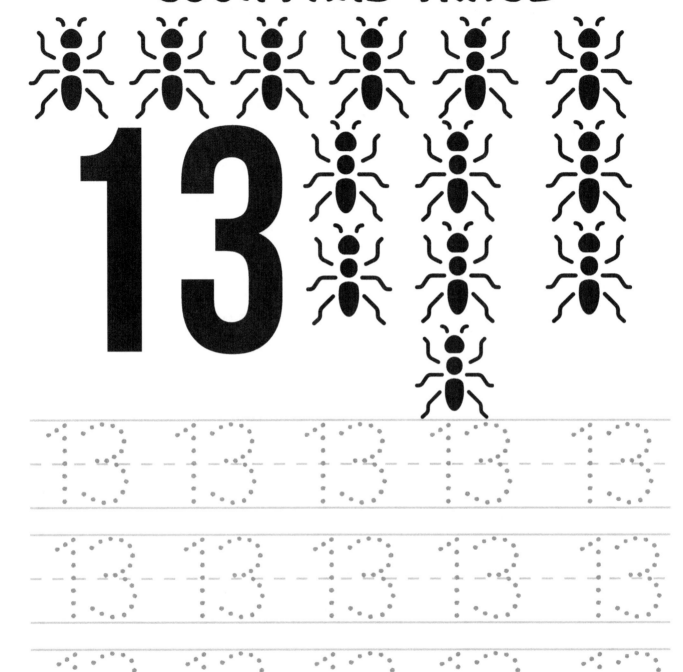

Spot The Differences

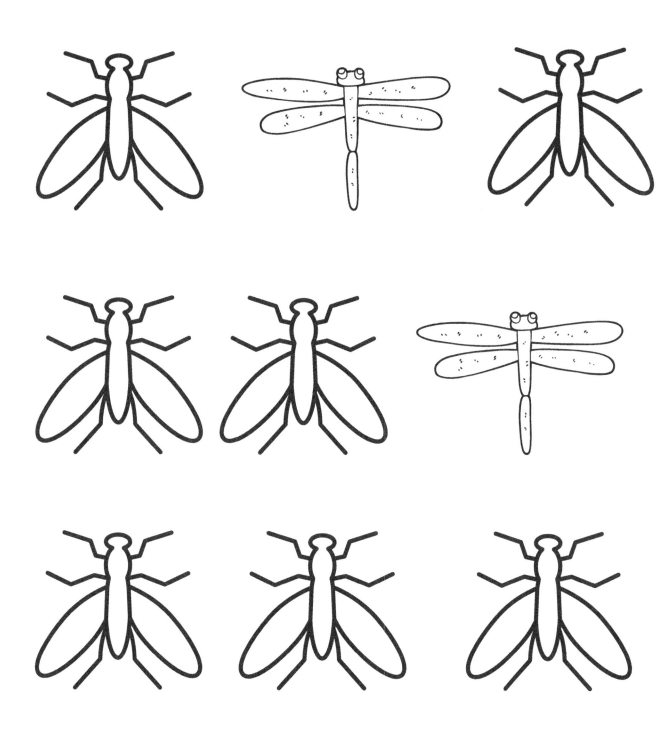

COUNT AND TRACE

14

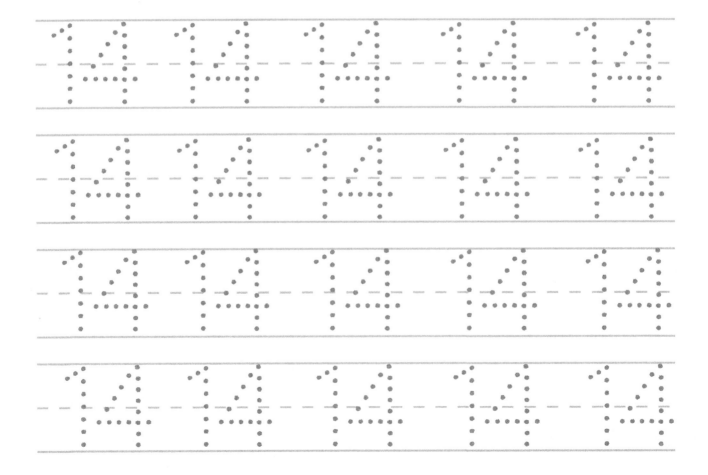

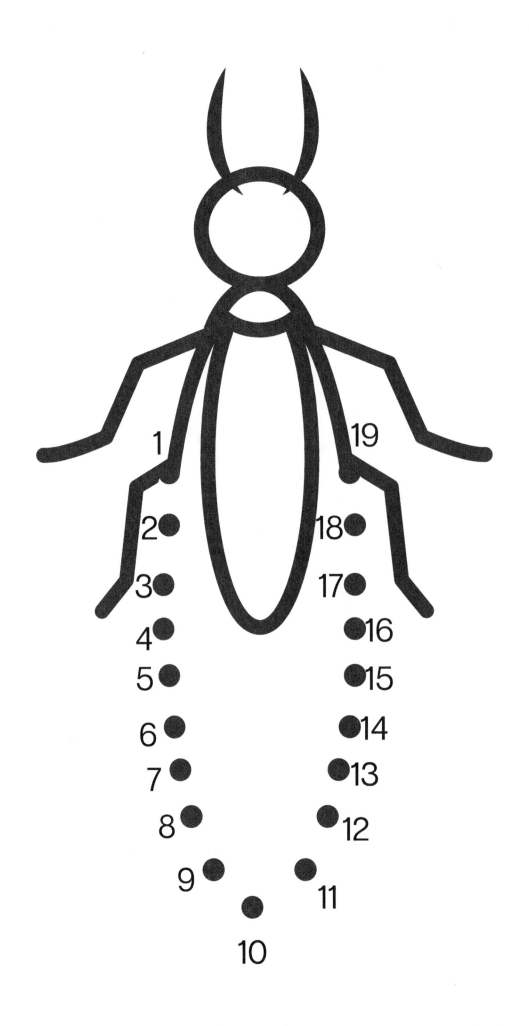

Help the bug through the maze.

Word Search

Circle The Words Below

```
Y  L  F  N  O  G  A  R  D
O  U  T  I  N  S  R  H  Y
U  D  U  U  H  N  C  D  F
R  I  N  T  E  N  M  A  L
E  F  T  T  R  E  O  S  T
H  M  P  S  H  T  I  W  W
O  H  P  U  R  A  N  M  B
G  U  T  J  A  G  T  A  R
C  G  O  C  G  L  A  T  E
```

moths   your

dragonfly   with

COUNT AND TRACE

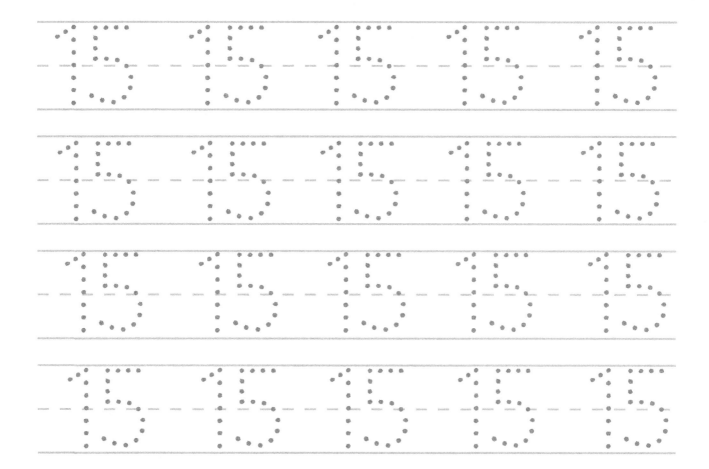

Spot The Difference

COUNT AND TRACE

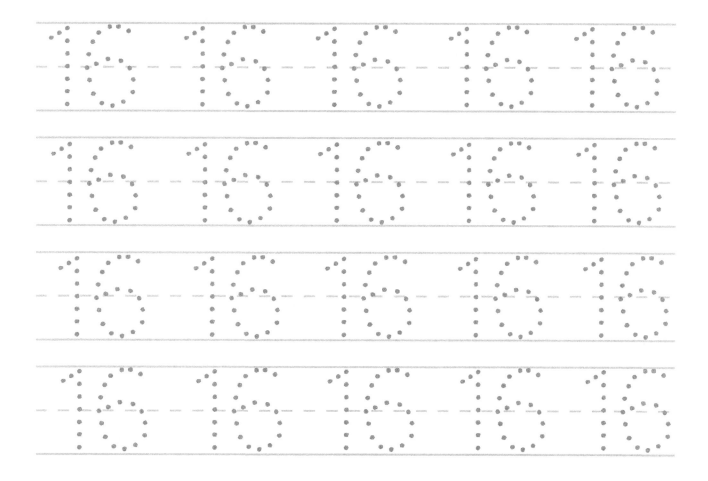

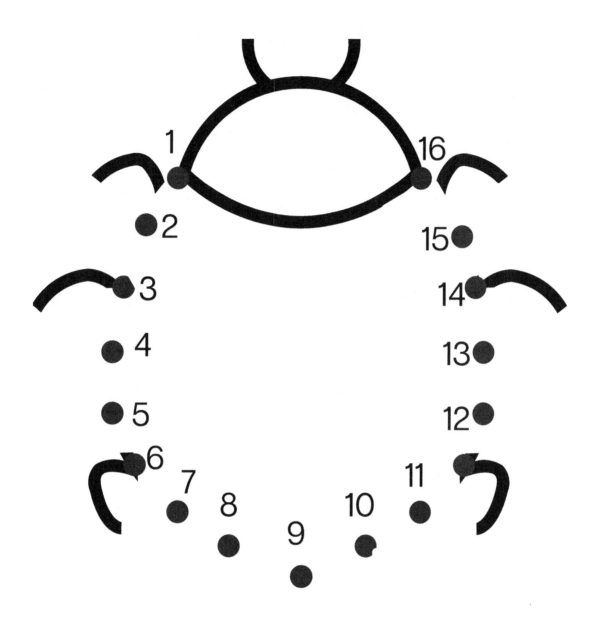

Help the bug through the maze.

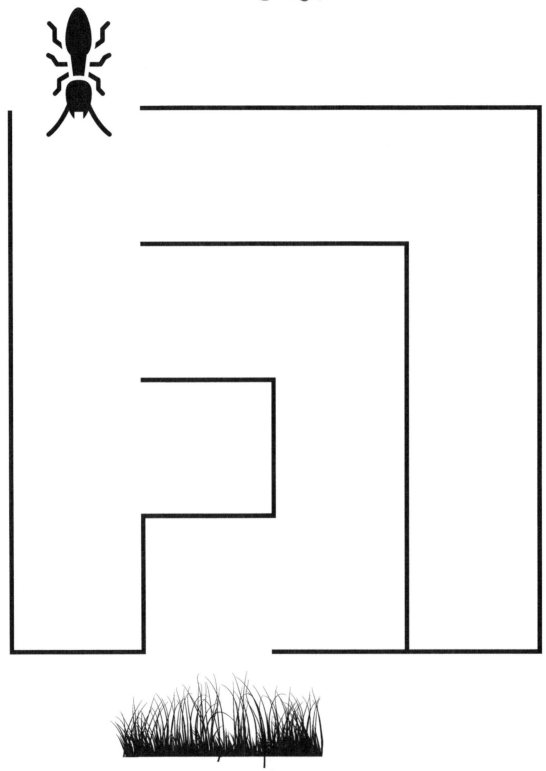

Word Search

Circle The Words Below

```
S  U  I  N  L  C  U  H  T
G  A  L  O  N  T  T  C  R
N  C  J  A  G  E  A  R  A
I  A  P  R  A  R  C  E  N
W  N  A  A  L  M  F  E  D
E  O  L  E  A  I  U  L  O
C  A  C  R  U  T  O  I  E
A  I  K  F  R  E  H  O  R
L  D  E  C  F  T  A  N  E
```

lacewings   termite

lice   and

COUNT AND TRACE

17

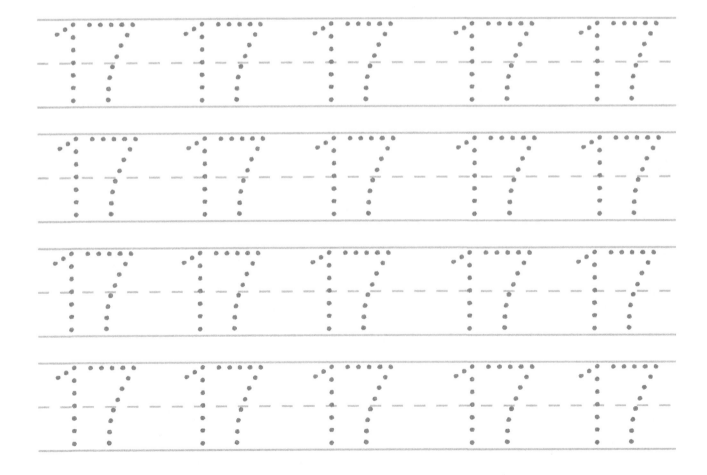

Spot The Differences

COUNT AND TRACE

18

18 18 18 18 18 18

18 18 18 18 18 18

19 19 19 19 19 19

18 18 18 18 18 18

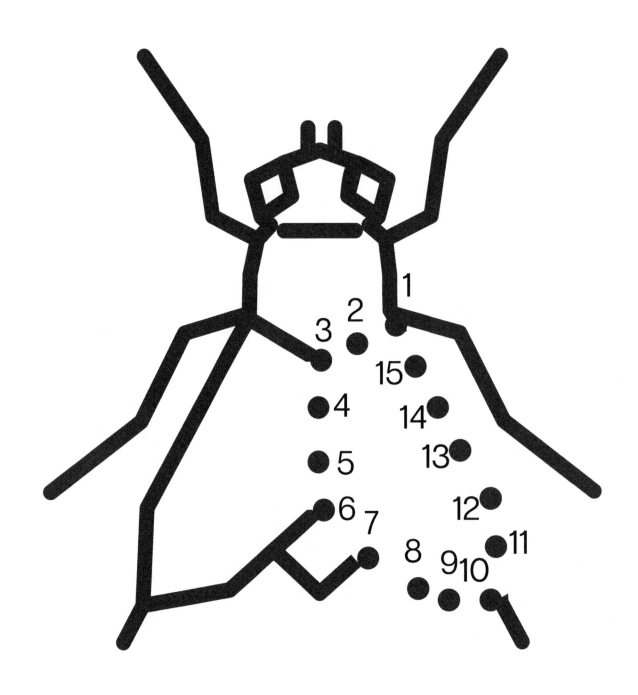

Help the bug through the maze.

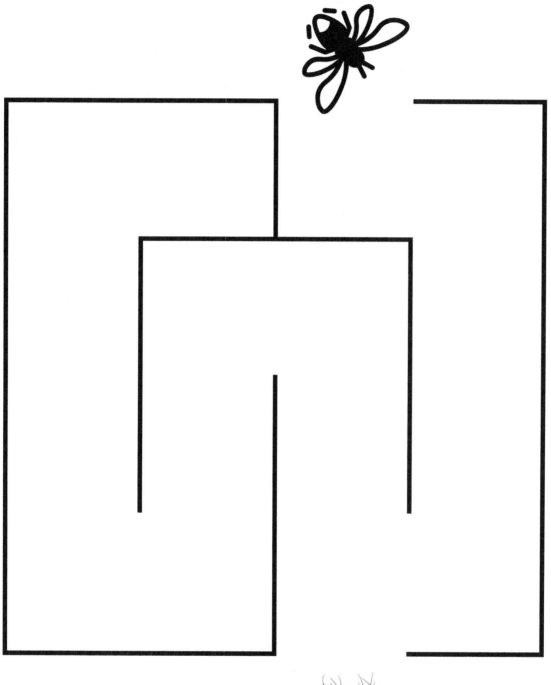

Word Search
Circle The Words Below

```
E  S  R  I  L  L  A  R  P
A  A  F  O  P  N  E  E  A
N  E  R  U  M  T  R  S  D
D  L  I  W  O  C  H  A  D
R  F  T  A  I  O  D  I  O
O  F  T  S  S  G  D  D  C
V  I  L  P  E  A  N  W  K
E  S  E  U  G  A  T  T  I
R  H  F  M  A  N  Y  T  E
```

earwig   wasp

fleas   said

COUNT AND TRACE

19

19 19 19 19 19 19

19 19 19 19 19 19

19 19 19 19 19 19

19 19 19 19 19 19

Spot The Differences

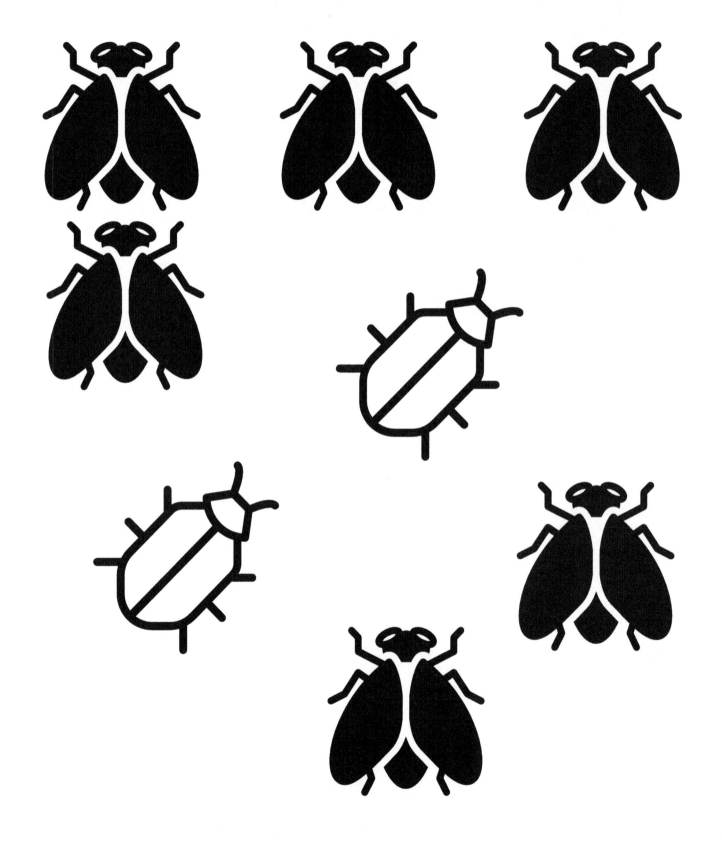

COUNT AND TRACE

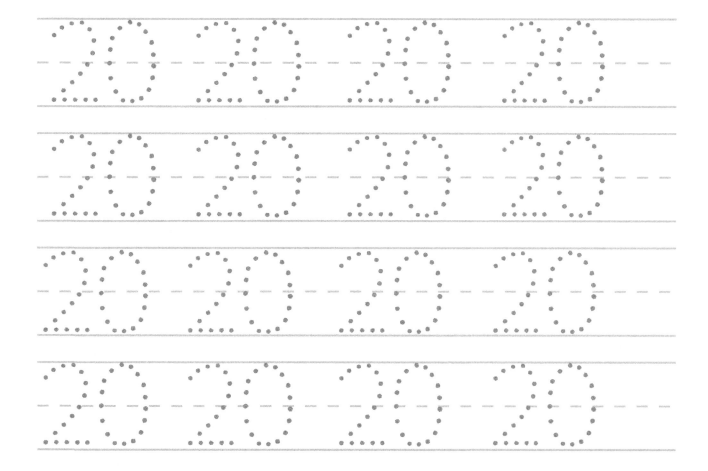

Help the bug
through the maze.

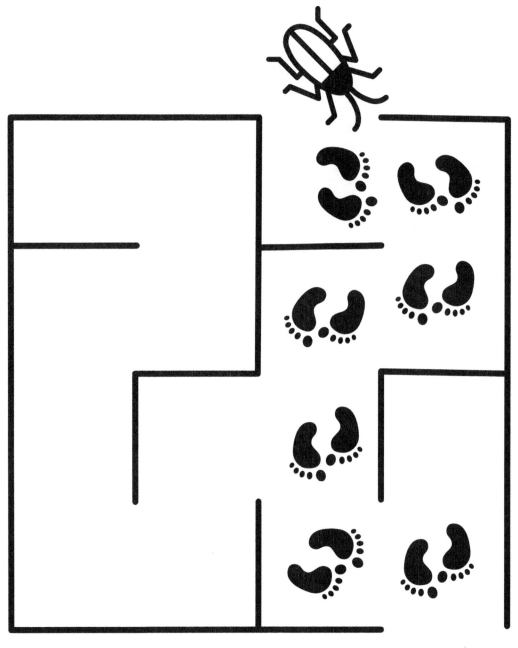

Word Search

Circle The Words Below

```
L U H N Y F U R T
N A E O P K G S D
A R D U W N L E F
D D A Y V I S L P
T R M I L T R D U
R D G A O S U D K
A C E H K U S A C
I U T U L E P S I
N H D C O R A T P
```

lady   made

stink   make

Spot The Difference

Help the bug
through the maze.

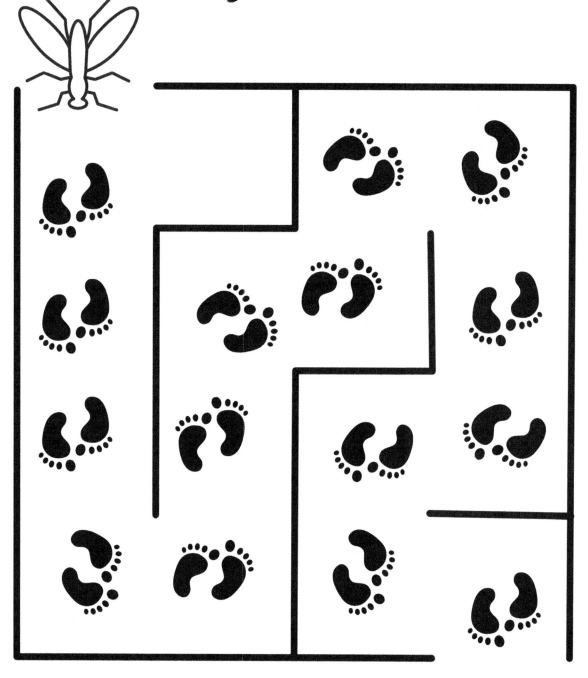

Word Search

Circle The Words Below

```
B U D N C L U R T
A S Q O S D P C B
S P H W E R E R A
N I A H O U T A R
D D F E E E E N N
O E T N E A U E A
C R E B F N N W L
K R R V L E T G O
C R I C K E T T E
```

spider   were

cricket   when

Spot The Difference

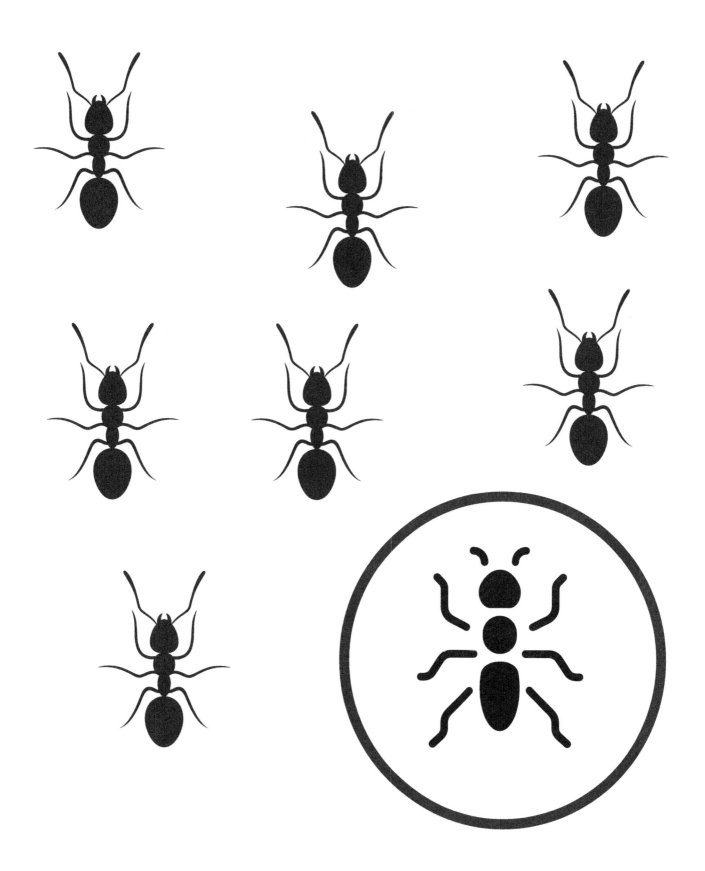

Help the bug through the maze.

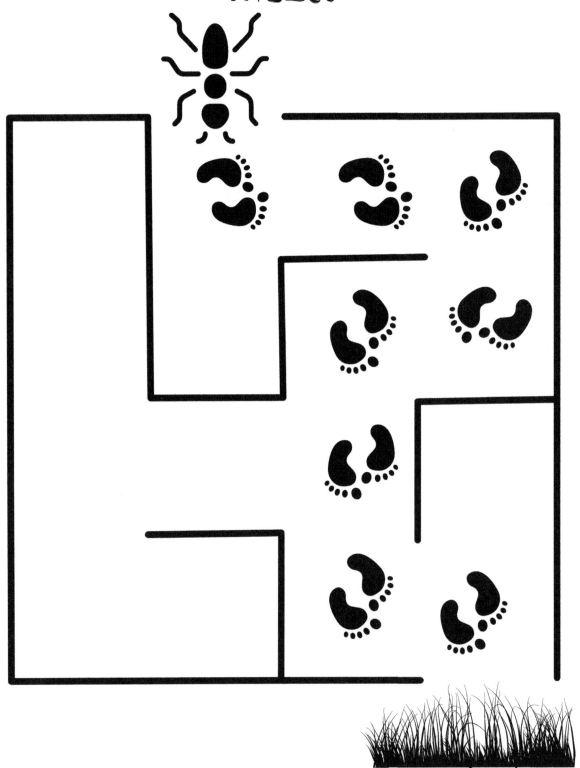

Word Search

Circle The Words Below

```
T U G N D F U R K
J O L E Y F I S C
S C E L L D L E O
G S N L F E H A T
R T E C N E D L S
A N E N I T L R E
S A B A R A U W V
S E A H O L O E I
C O H C I H W T L
```

ants   which

seed   would

Spot The Differences

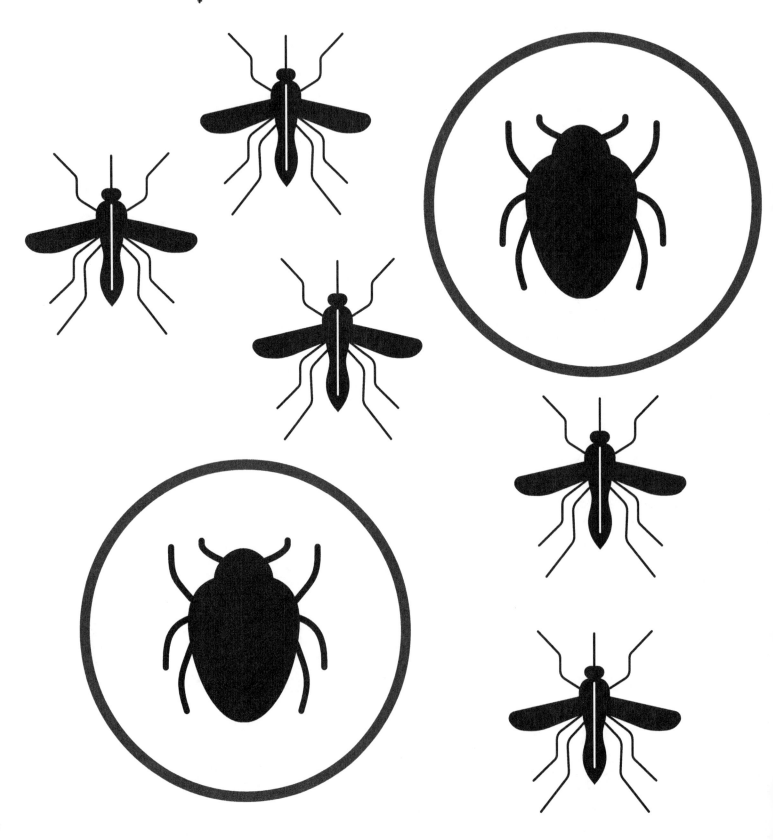

Help the bug
through the maze.

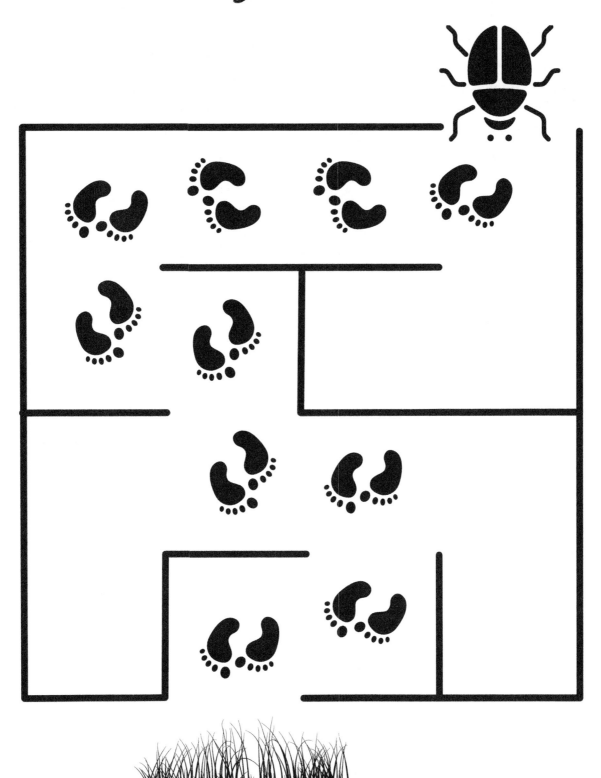

Word Search

Circle The Words Below

```
S  W  G  N  Y  F  U  R  B  B
B  I  X  O  R  L  E  R  I
F  L  L  U  U  E  L  I  S
L  P  N  V  E  O  E  N  O
Y  D  O  E  E  P  I  N  N
A  D  E  R  L  R  C  D  W
R  F  N  Y  R  O  P  W  E
K  U  L  O  R  W  T  T  R
C  H  D  C  F  N  A  T  E
```

fly

very

silver

use

Spot The Difference

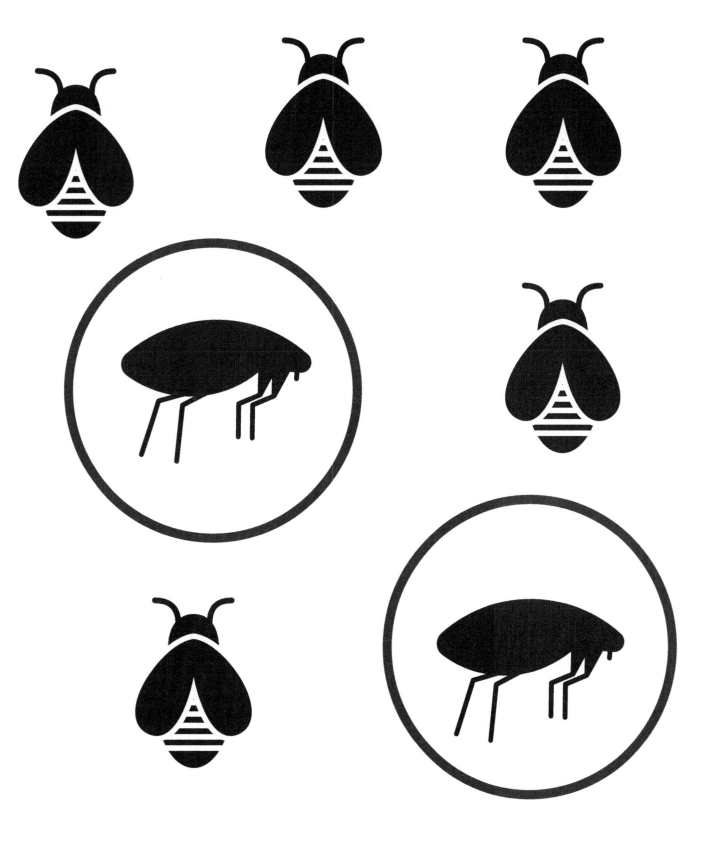

Help the bug through the maze.

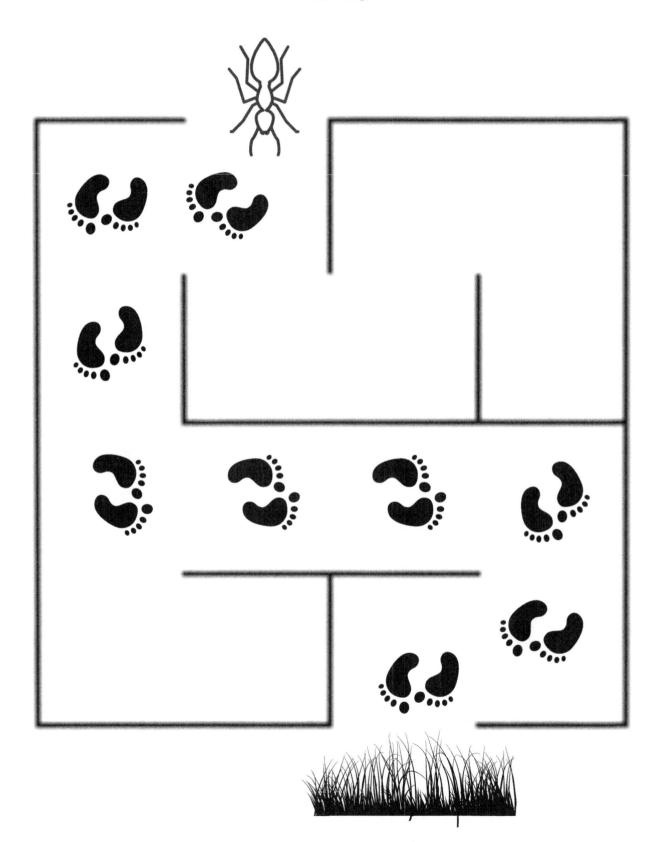

Word Search

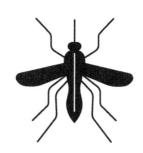

Circle The Words Below

```
P  S  W  H  H  I  N  O  C
A  A  F  C  P  N  E  E  O
G  G  N  A  E  T  M  A  C
N  A  A  B  I  T  E  R  H
O  F  E  E  L  U  R  L  R
L  O  P  D  B  B  F  O  O
C  X  Y  I  I  E  N  W  A
K  U  T  R  N  A  P  G  C
G  A  R  B  A  A  G  E  H
```

bed   bite

cockroach   long

Spot The Difference

Help the bug
through the maze.

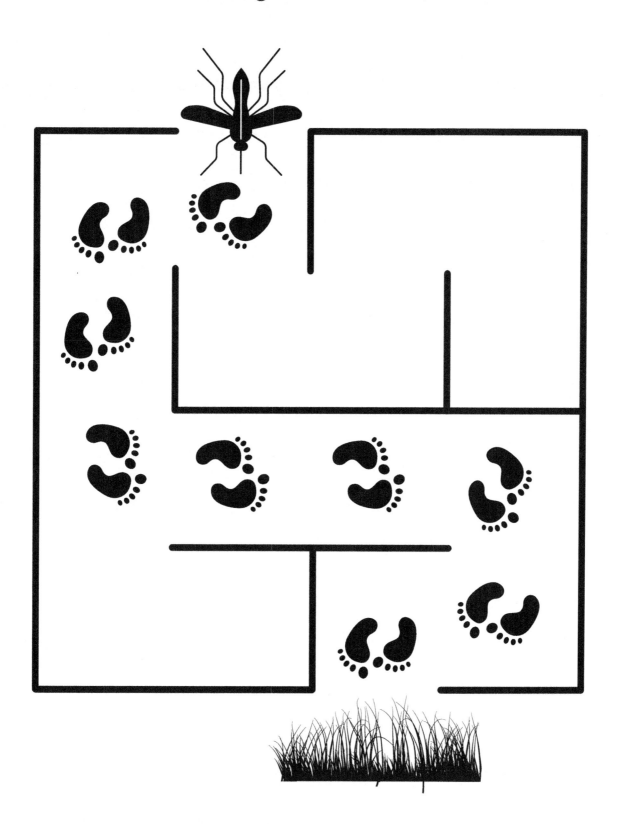

Word Search

Circle The Words Below

```
C E N T I P E D E E
R C A H F I N D H
E M A E I A Y I E
S A A B R L R Y E
S N R E S R E B T
A C A E T H R O A
G L C A T S T L H
E U N A D E S A R
C P F R T Y U T H
```

centipede   the

bee   they

Spot The Difference

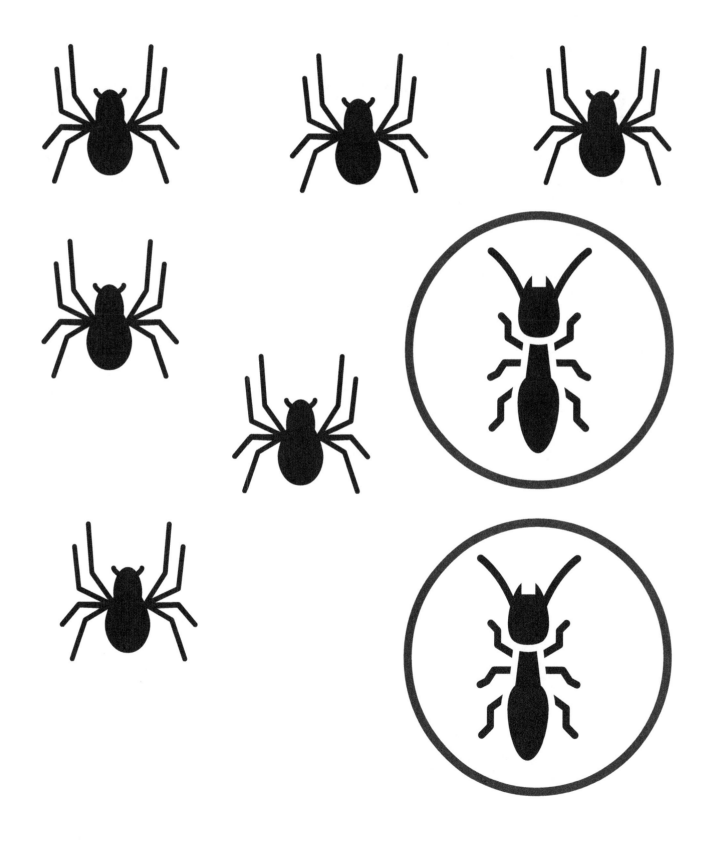

Help the bug through the maze.

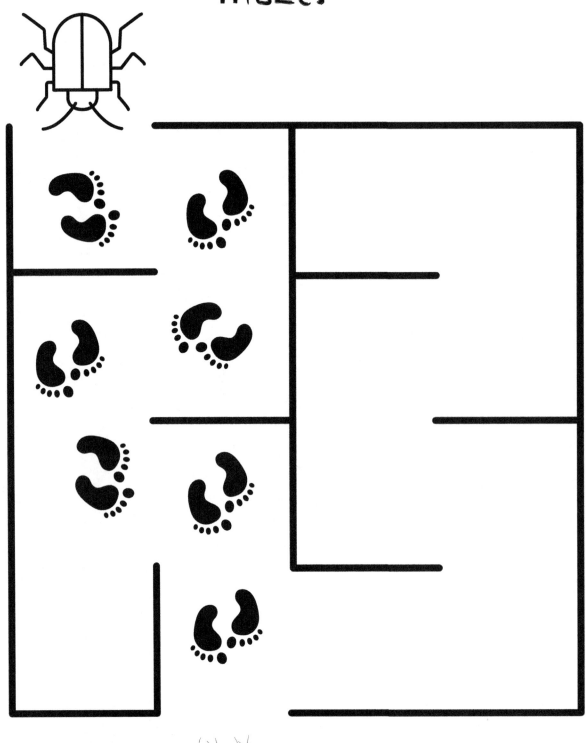

Word Search

Circle The Words Below

M	I	S	E	L	T	E	E	B
O	S	F	R	P	W	E	F	U
G	A	I	T	B	E	E	T	T
I	W	N	R	F	E	T	N	T
R	N	A	R	A	V	I	B	E
T	O	O	S	L	I	L	O	R
H	I	N	F	P	L	I	W	F
G	F	A	I	D	S	T	G	L
C	H	D	T	O	R	Y	L	Y

wasps   beetles

weevils   butterfly

Spot The Differences

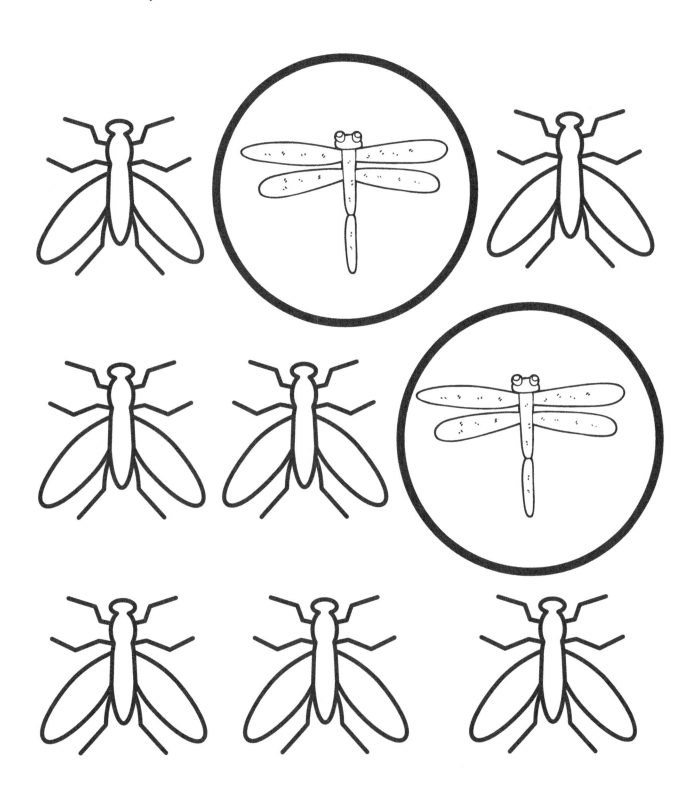

Help the bug through the maze.

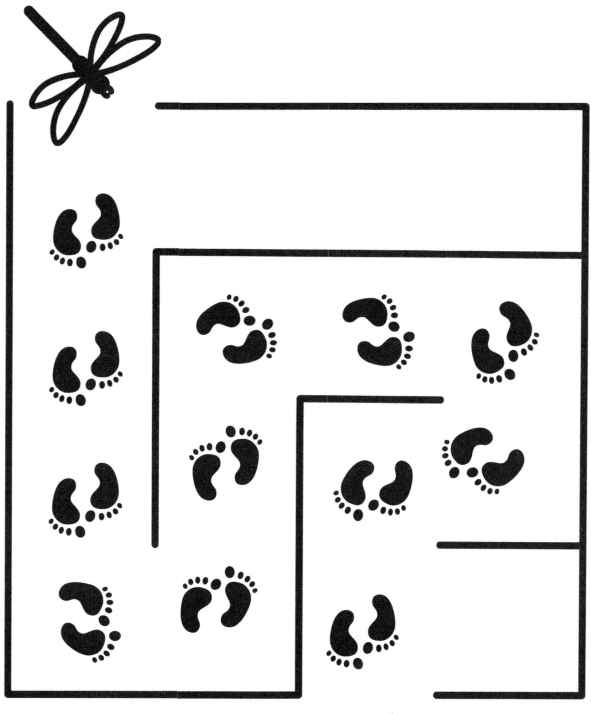

Word Search

Circle The Words Below

```
Y L F N O G A R D
O U T I N S R H Y
U D U U H N C D F
R I N T E N M A L
E F T T R E O S T
H M P S H T I W W
O H P U R A N M B
G U T J A G T A R
C G O C G L A T E
```

moths   your

dragonfly   with

Spot The Difference

Help the bug through the maze.

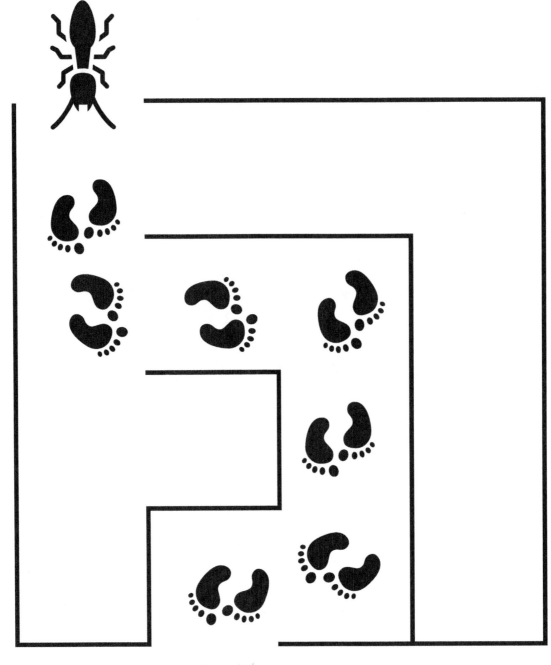

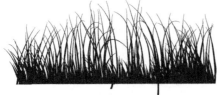

Word Search

Circle The Words Below

```
S  U  I  N  L  C  U  H  T
G  A  L  O  N  T  T  C  R
N  C  J  A  G  E  A  R  A
I  A  P  R  A  R  C  E  N
W  N  A  A  L  M  F  E  D
E  O  L  E  A  I  U  L  O
C  A  C  R  U  T  O  I  E
A  I  K  F  R  E  H  O  R
L  D  E  C  F  T  A  N  E
```

lacewings   termite

lice   and

Spot The Differences

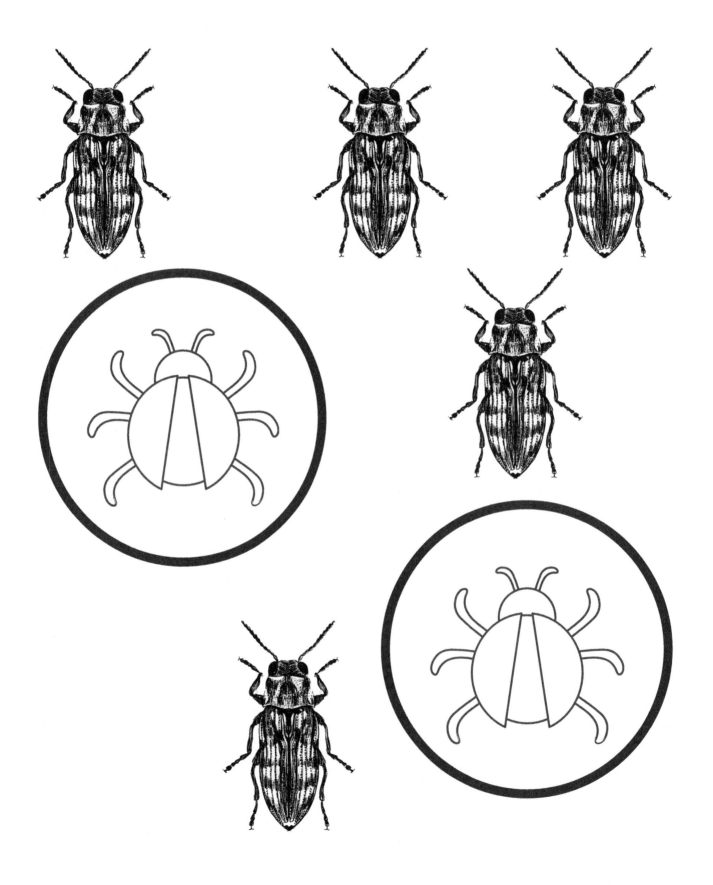

Help the bug through the maze.

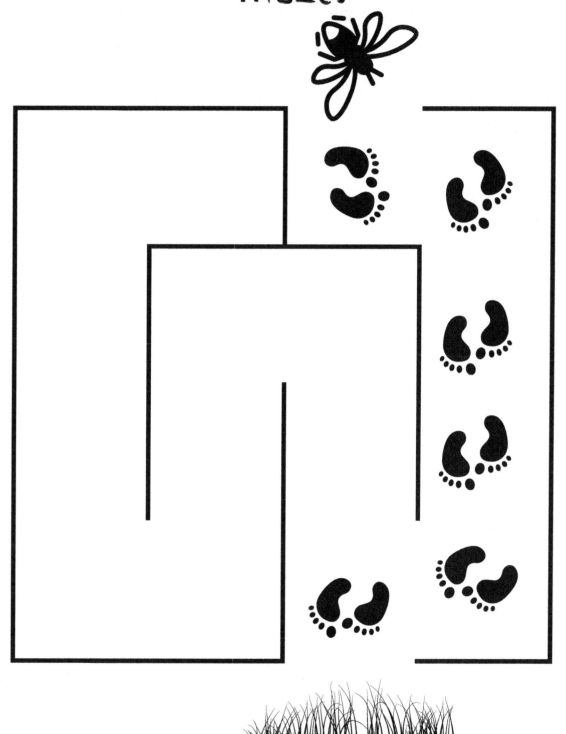

Word Search

Circle The Words Below

E S R I L L A R P P
A A F O P N E E A
N E R U M T R S D
D L I W O C H A D
R F I T A I O D I O
O F T S S G D D C
V I L P E A N W K
E S E U G A T T I
R H F M A N Y T E

earwig

wasp

fleas

said

Spot The Differences

Printed in Great Britain
by Amazon

39629987R00057